Contemporary Traditions
In Native American Pottery

Contemporary Traditions examines the evolution of traditional Native American art forms and designs into contemporary forms and designs.

Native American artists, while working to preserve the cultural traditions embodied in their art, are enhancing these traditional art forms and designs with new shapes, new patterns, and new techniques.

This book focuses on the innovative designs found in lids, slips and glazes, fanciful figures, and adornments found on Southwest Native American pottery.

Art always pushes the envelope — art always evolves.

Innovation

Pottery is one of the oldest human inventions originating some 30,000 to 40,000 years ago. As early as 29,000 B.C. animal and human figurines were made from clay and fired in pits dug into the ground. About 10,000 years later people began using pottery for utilitarian and functional purposes. Native American pottery has been made as far back as 300 B.C. It is one of the major identifying characteristics of the Southwestern Pueblo Indians.

Most of the Pueblo Native Americans today use the same basic technology of pottery-making they have for centuries. They gather the raw materials, clean and crush them, and add any tempering agent that may be needed. The clay is then hand coiled into beautiful jars, ollas, and other unique shapes. After polishing and applying a slip or glaze, the pieces are fired in outdoor pits.

Many contemporary artists are pushing the boundaries and adding innovative touches, designs, colors, or appliques to their pottery. They are creating contemporary traditions.

The Difficult Art of Lids

Jars and pots with lids are an elevated art form due to the difficulty of creating the perfect lid for a piece of pottery.

Because they are flat, lids tend to warp and shrink as they dry. It is only a very masterful potter who can achieve this level of degree of innovative difficulty.

This three sectioned jar is capped with a perfectly seated lid elevating it to a higher level of innovation. Lids are extremely difficult to achieve. It requires masterful carving to create a lid which not only enhances a piece of pottery, but one that fits securely on the piece.

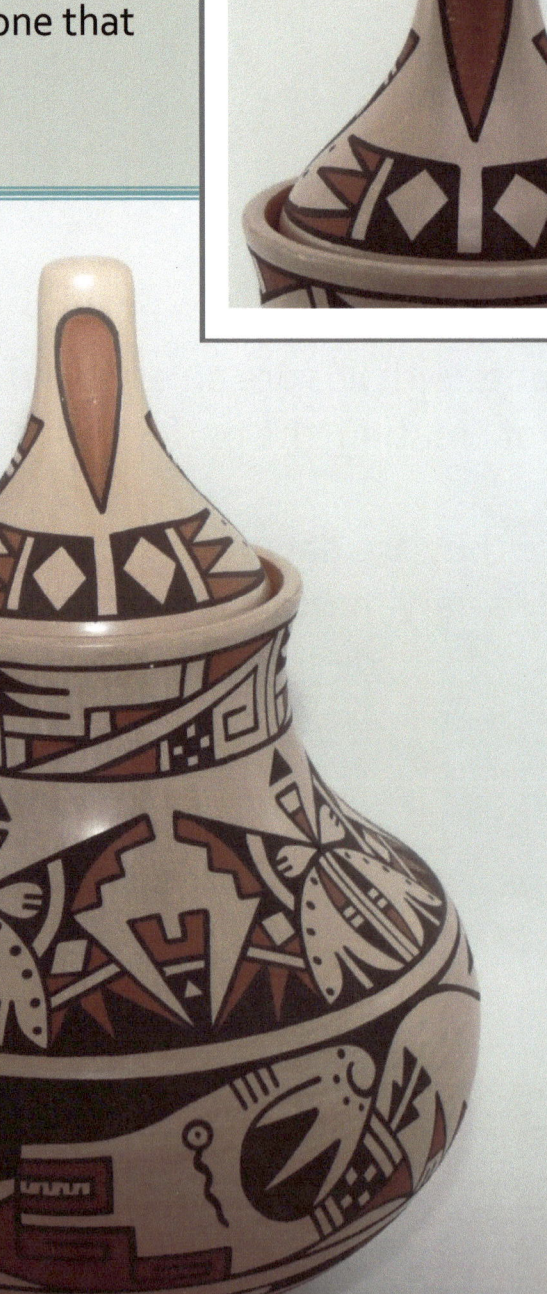

Erik Fender
Than Tsideh (Sunbird)
San Ildefonso Pueblo.

The lid, topped with a scalloped shell, combines the use of two colors of clay. This lid fits expertly on the outside of the top of the pot. The matte finish of the shell, as the knob, juxtaposes with the highly polished fitted portion of the lid. This is a example of an innovative method of texture and color.

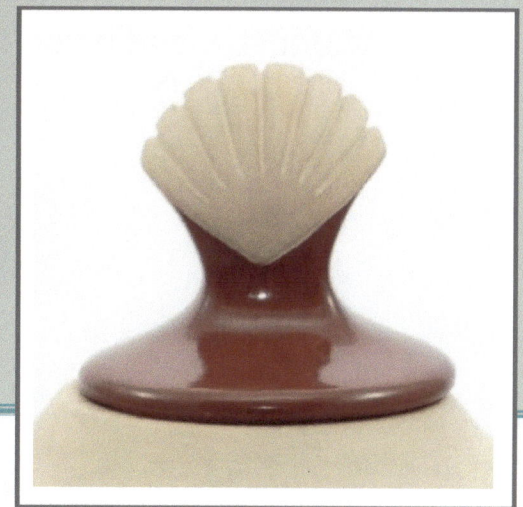

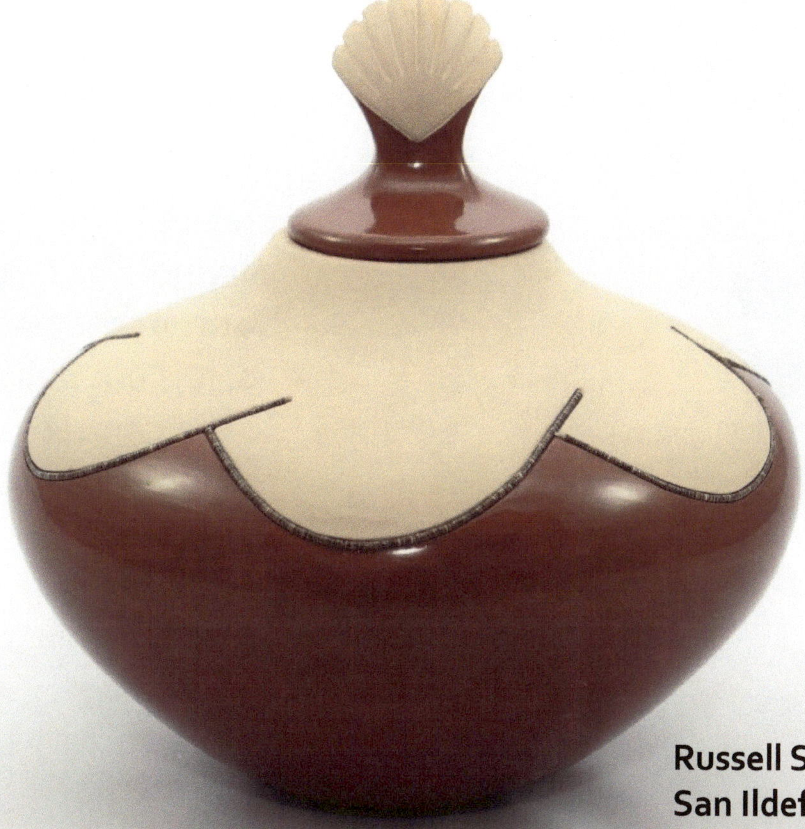

Russell Sanchez
San Ildefonso Pueblo

Animal sculptures atop of pottery are quite unusual and give the pottery a unique art form.

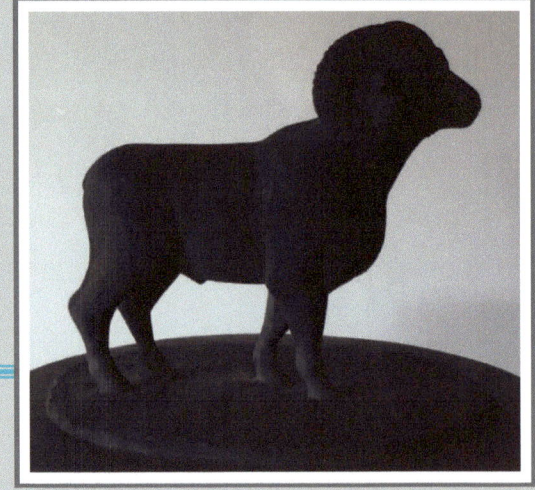

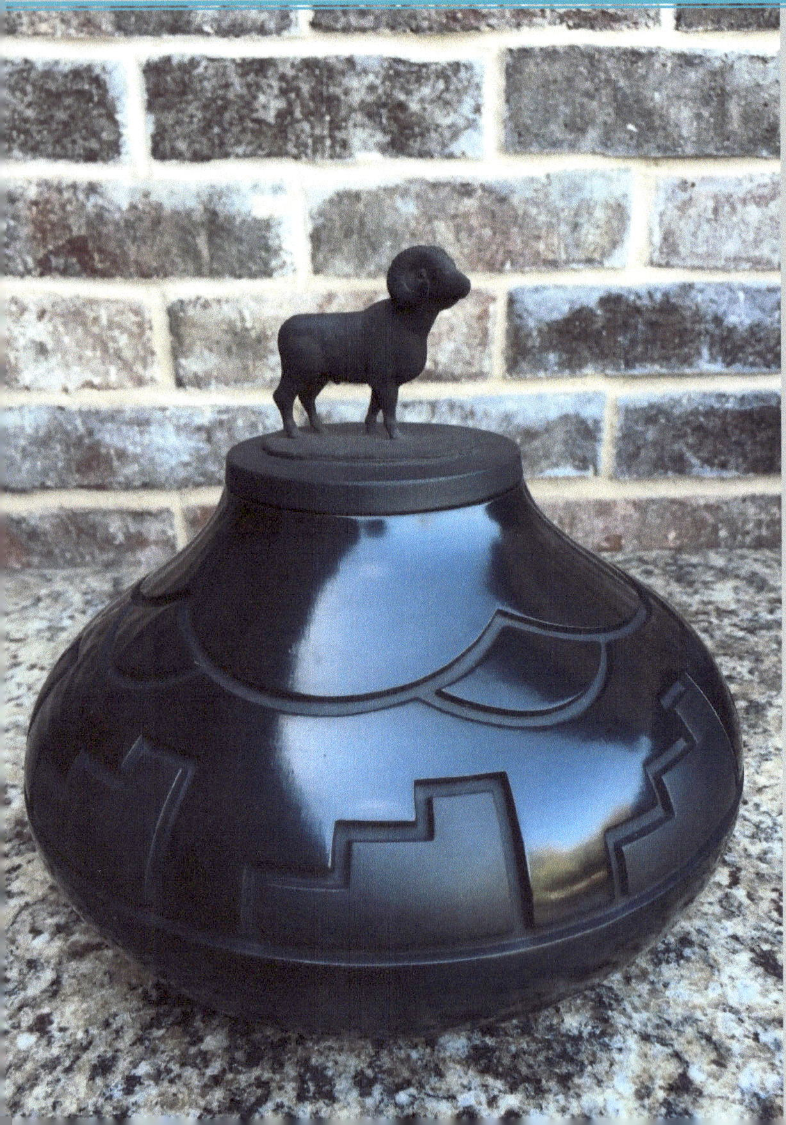

These figural lids require a precise hand in shaping and carving. The ram on this lid is of a soft matte finish, and like the lid, it is not polished, which adds to the contrast and emphasizes the innovation of the piece.

Jeff Roller
Santa Clara Pueblo

The lid on this tall cylinder has been so carefully crafted as to sit entirely inside the jar. This innovative technique is quite difficult to master, for the lid must fit precisely while being absolutely flat.

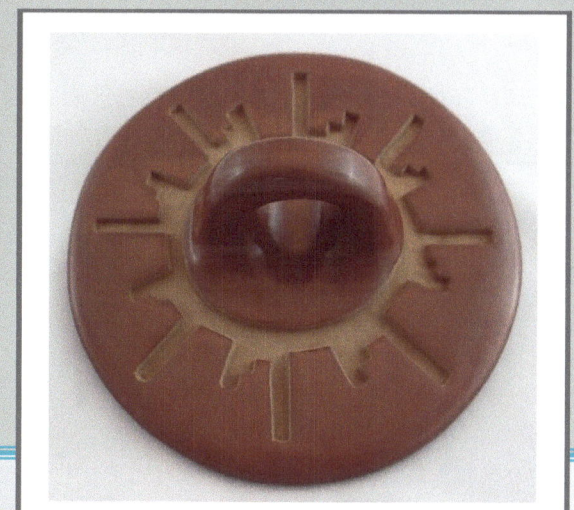

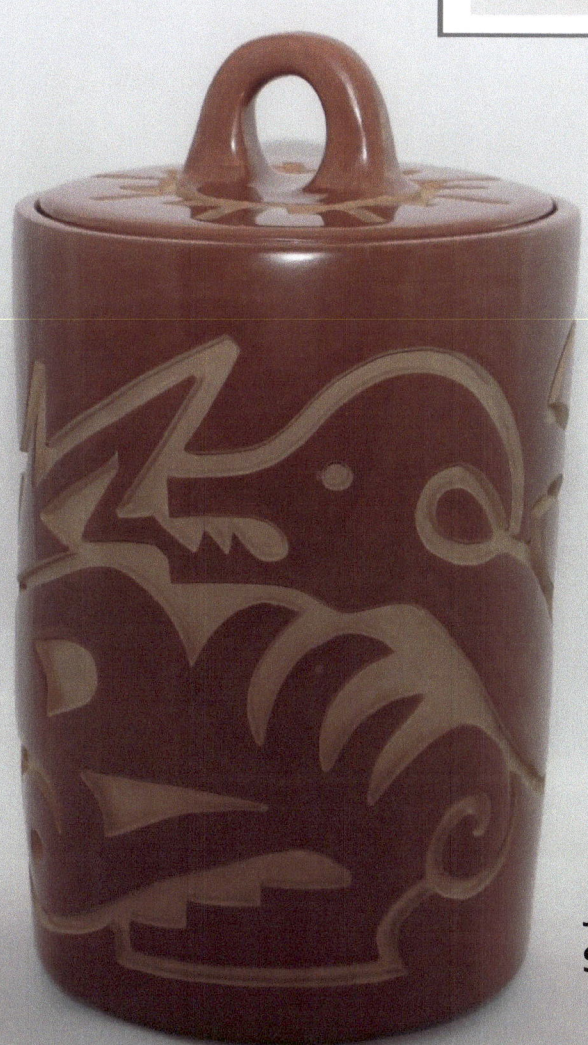

Jason Ebelacker
Santa Clara Pueblo

Special Slips and Glazes

Slips and glazes are applied to a piece of pottery during polishing to enhance the color, the shine and the designs.

Innovative potters are pushing the edge with new materials and new colors in unusual ways.

The green clay slip was responsible for the green color of this piece of San Ildefonso pottery.

The green slip was to have fired buff, instead it stayed green.

That green color is where innovation can happen in traditional pottery.

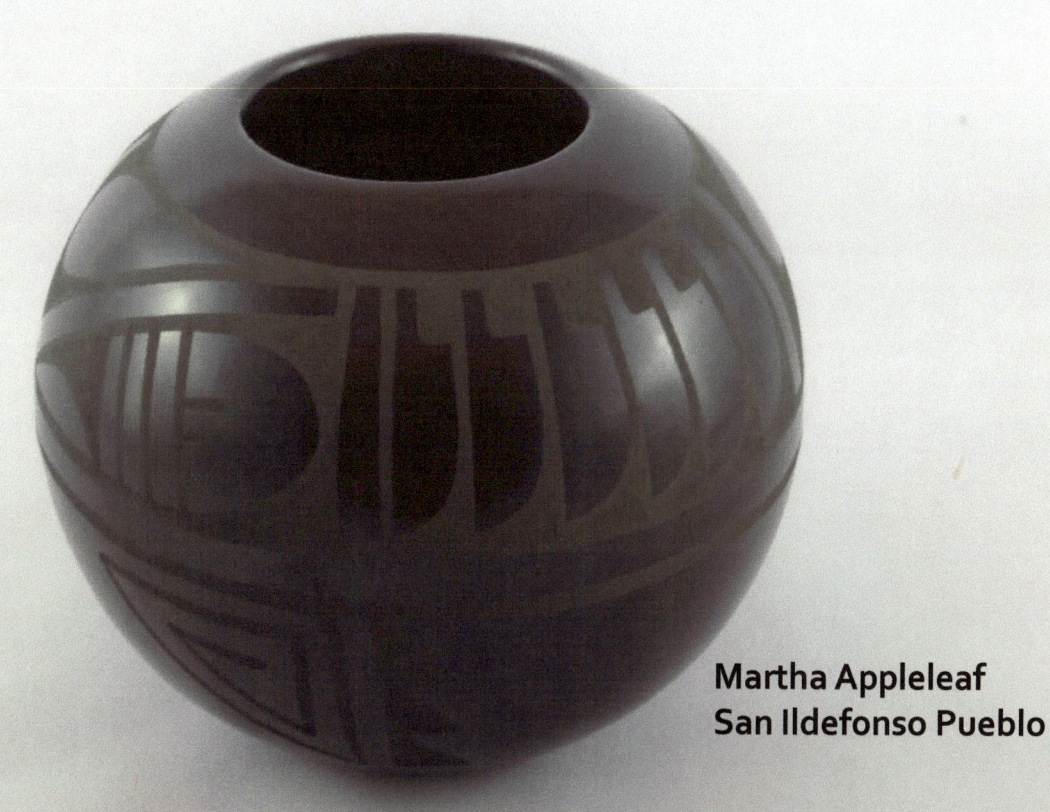

Martha Appleleaf
San Ildefonso Pueblo

The interesting result from some grease intruding into the firing process takes on a misty cloud like pattern of subtle warm, pale golds and soft greys as it combines with the white clay for a serene and sophisticated look that is truly unique.

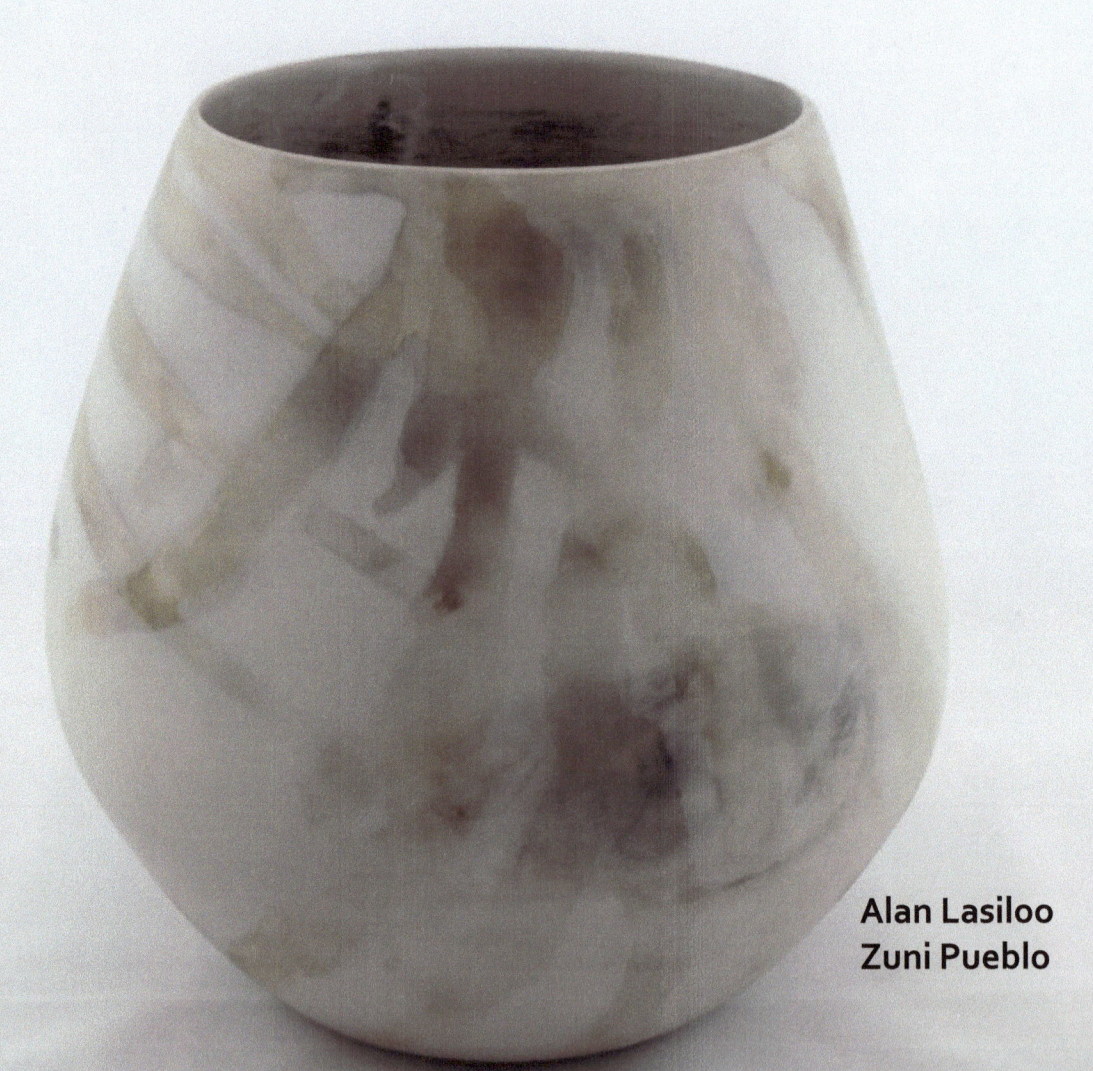

Alan Lasiloo
Zuni Pueblo

A new and unusual combination of glittering micaceous slip and matte finish make this jar seem to glow when it catches the light.

The upper and lower body sections are covered with a beautiful micaceous slip giving a shimmery effect to the pottery.

The body expertly shaped and smoothed has a matte finish. The mid section has four panels of rainbows and birds with corn.

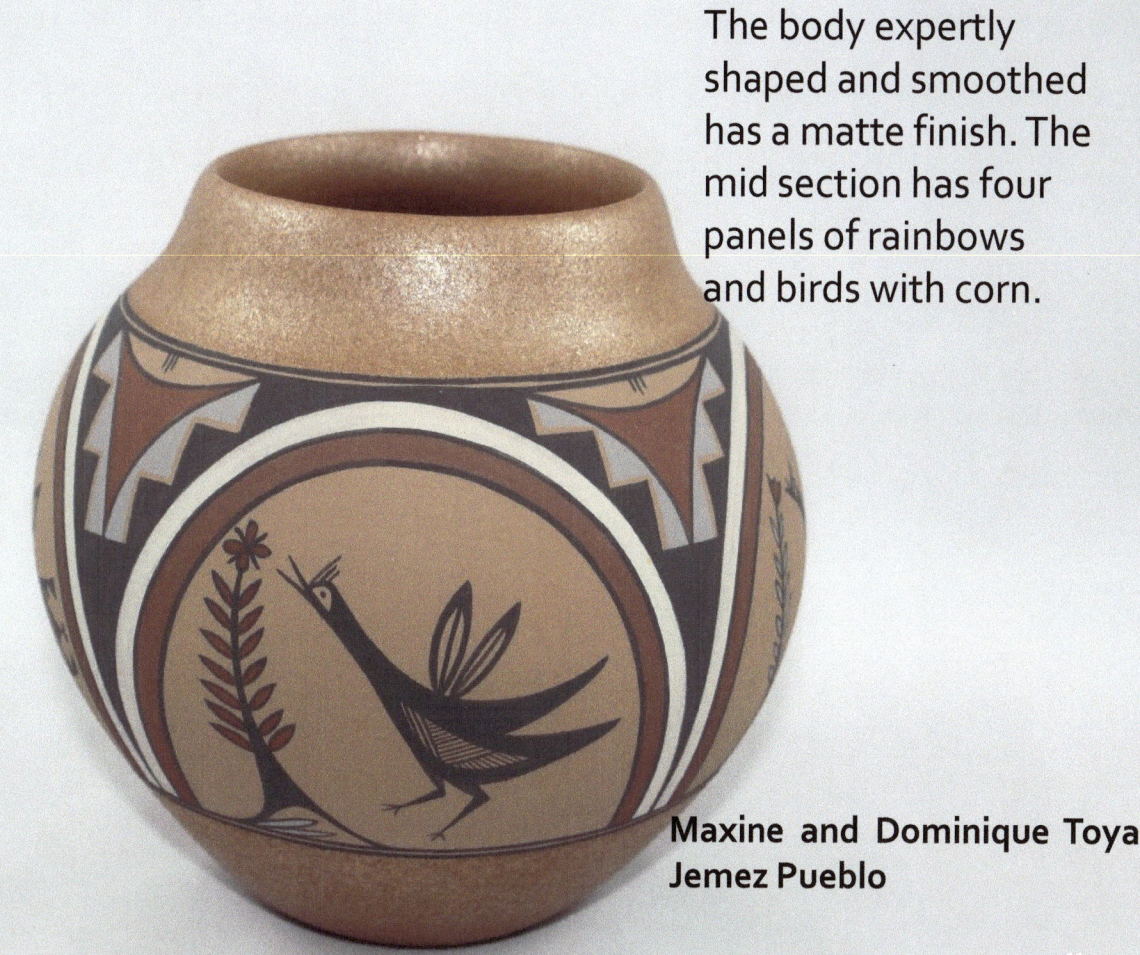

Maxine and Dominique Toya
Jemez Pueblo

Unique Designs

Collected by hand, ground and steeped, vegetal and mineral paints create the most interesting and unique patterns on Native American pottery.

Today's Laguna pottery is more geometric in design. Originally, Laguna pottery was very similar to that of Acoma with rainbow bands and birds.

A very small group of artists, including Stacy Carr and Myron Sarracino, continue to create fine pieces in the traditional manner painted with very intricate geometric patterns requiring a very steady hand and a delicate touch.

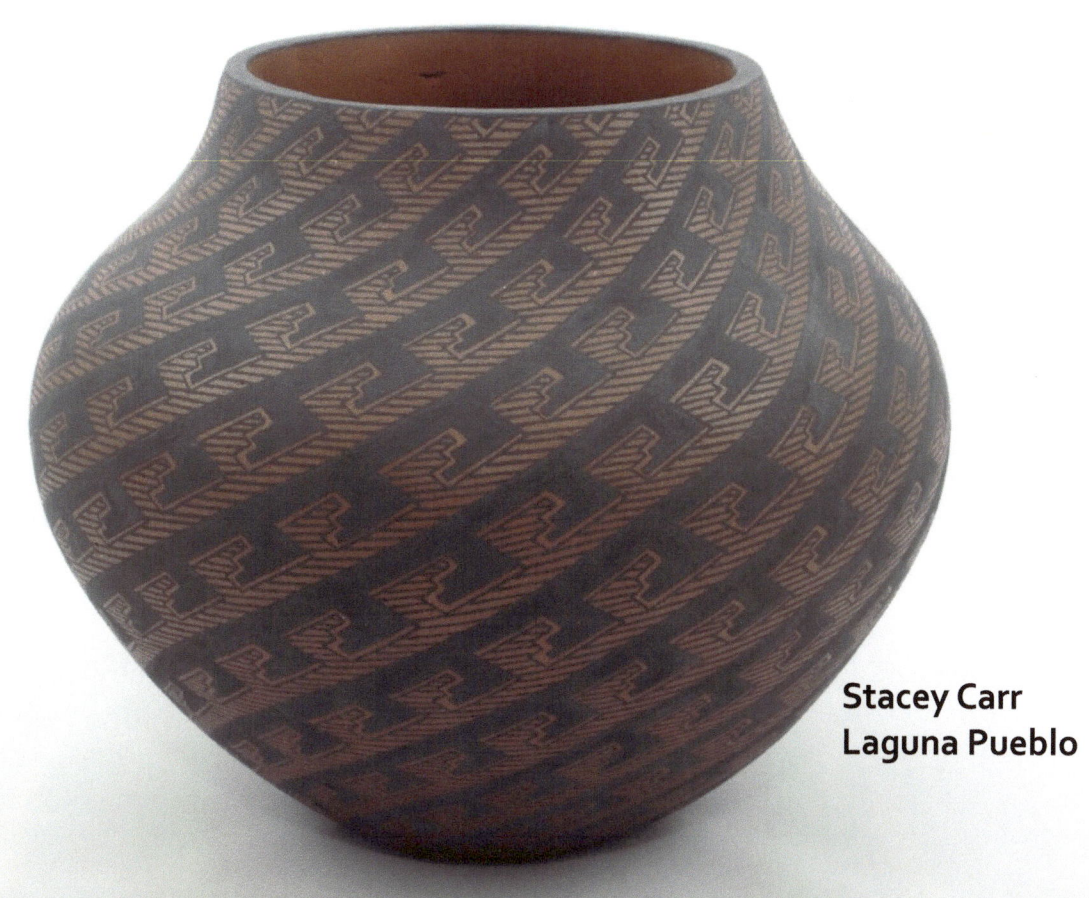

Stacey Carr
Laguna Pueblo

Another example, using a white pot with the painting being in a brown slip to give the impression of feathers.

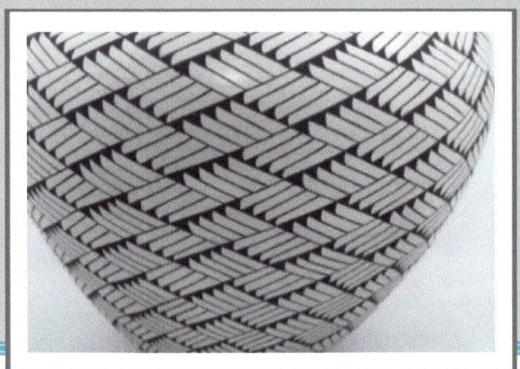

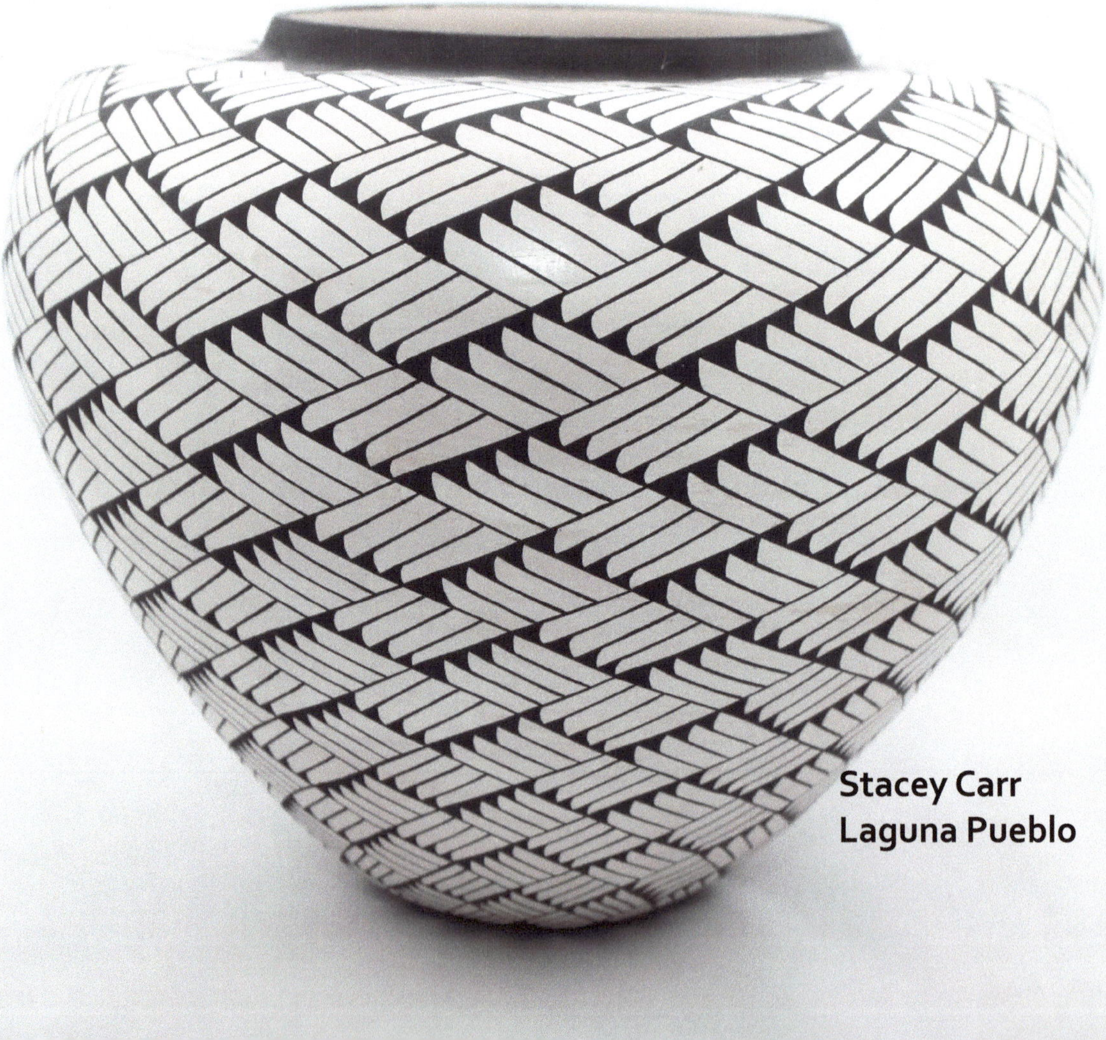

**Stacey Carr
Laguna Pueblo**

One-of-a-kind sgraffito designs enhance modern pottery. The art of sgraffito (in Italian "to scratch") is a pottery decorating technique that has been used for generations.

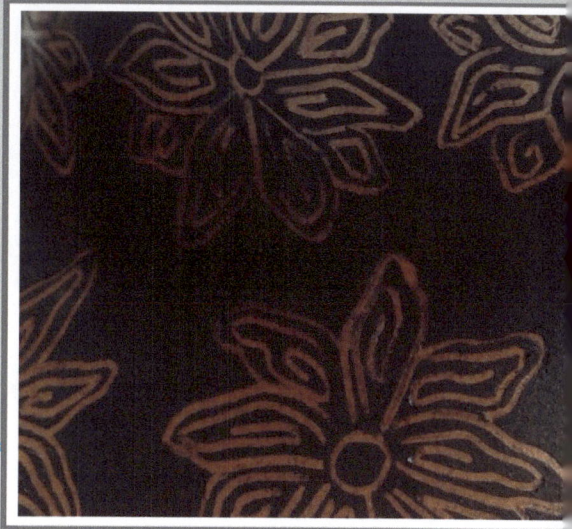

What is new and innovative is the type of sgraffito designs used by Karin Walkingstick. These techniques echo her Cherokee culture.

Karin Walkingstick
Cherokee

The use of sgraffito as an outline deign enhances the finely ground mussel shells in the clay adding a unique approach to this snake jar.

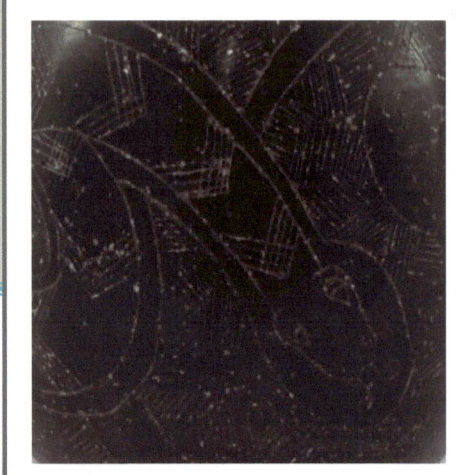

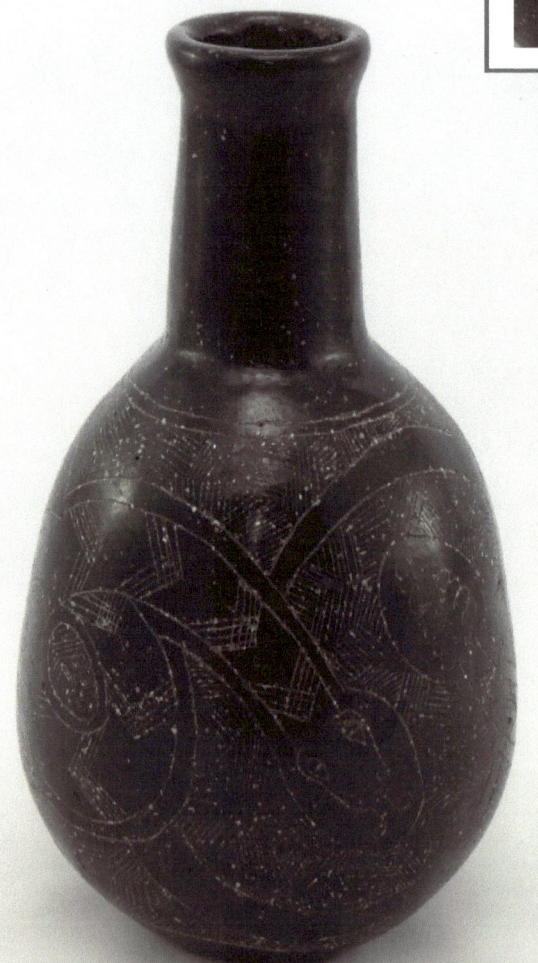

Chase Kahwinhut Earles
Caddo

Bold beautiful lines of intricate geometric designs give this large Laguna jar a very unique look – very contemporary although evocative of the past.

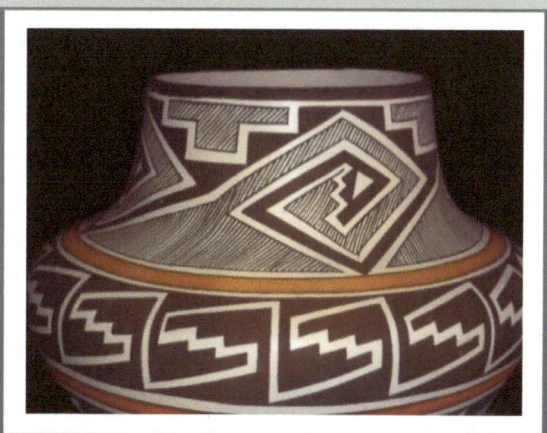

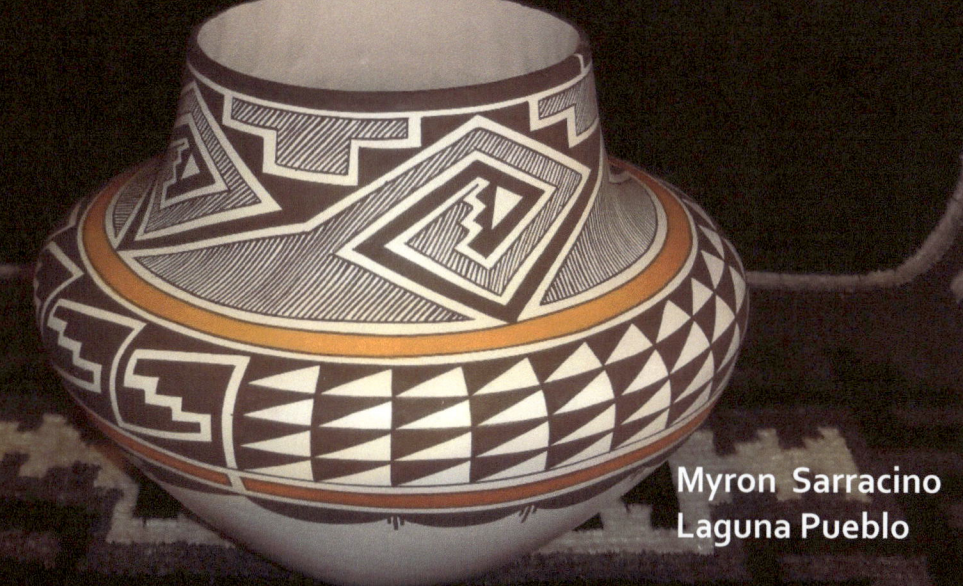

Myron Sarracino
Laguna Pueblo

Adornments and Appliques

Innovative motifs include a variety of appliquéd and incised plant and animal designs, as well as turquoise and handmade gold beads—usually in high relief and occasionally in full round.

The undulating insets of turquoise and handmade gold beads add a unique applique to the contrast of high polish and matte finish on this bowl.

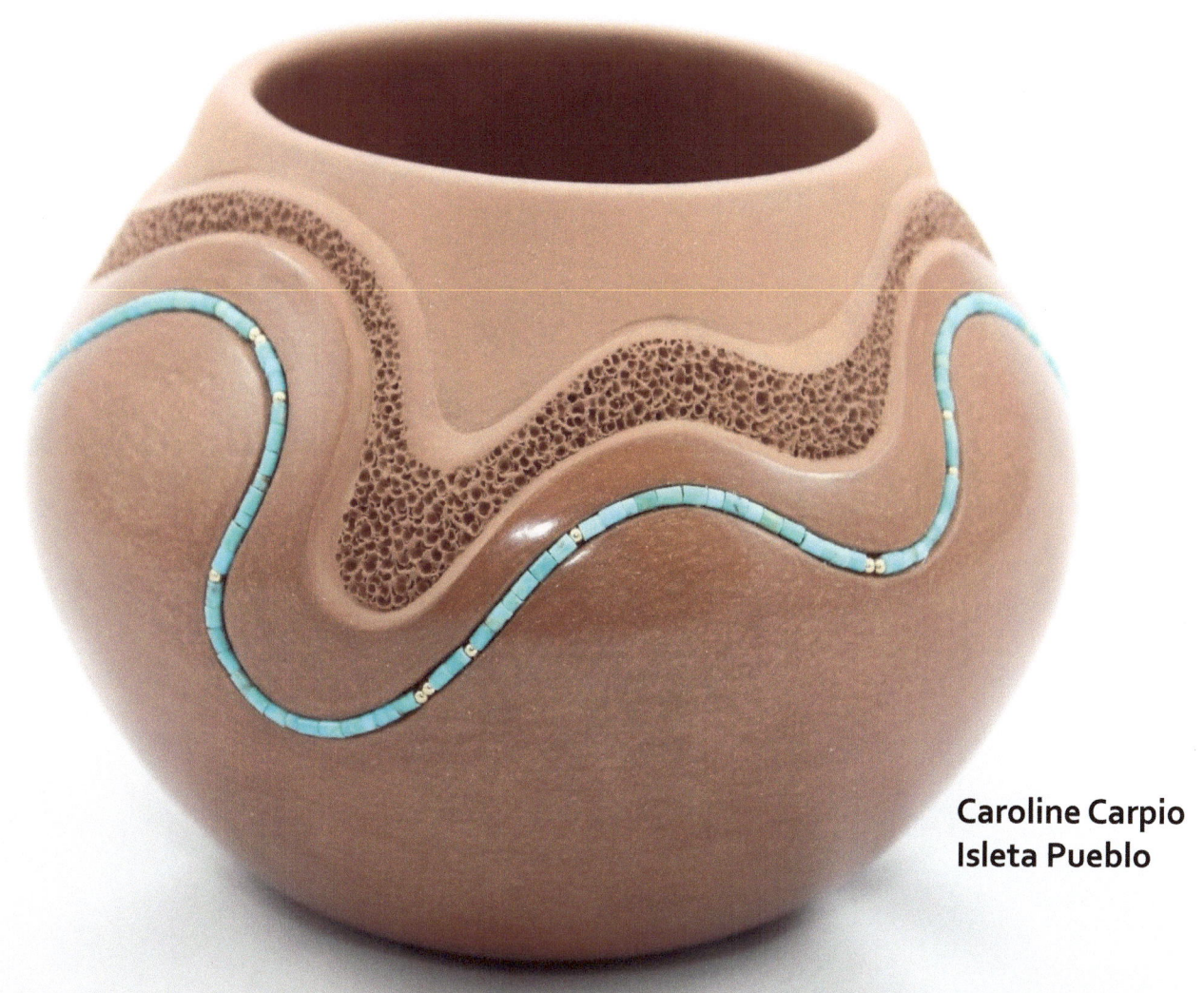

Caroline Carpio
Isleta Pueblo

The addition of the stacked representational pueblo adds a 3D dimension to the sculpture.

This juxtaposition of a soft matte finish with a highly polished shine increases the dramatic effect.

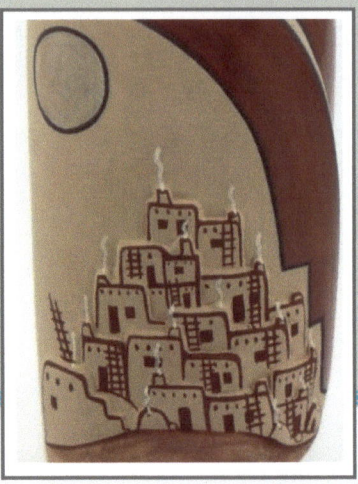

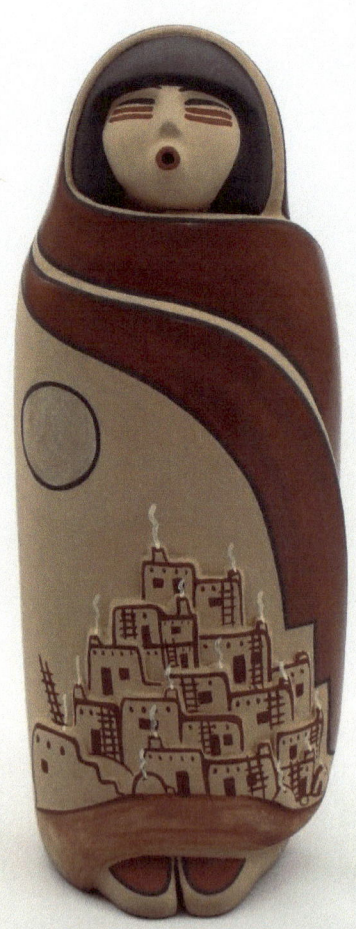

Maxine Toya
Jemez Pueblo

The additions of applique animals, insects and other designs are a recent innovation to Navajo pottery. The pitcher features corn, while the bowl features horned toads.

Elsie Black   Navajo

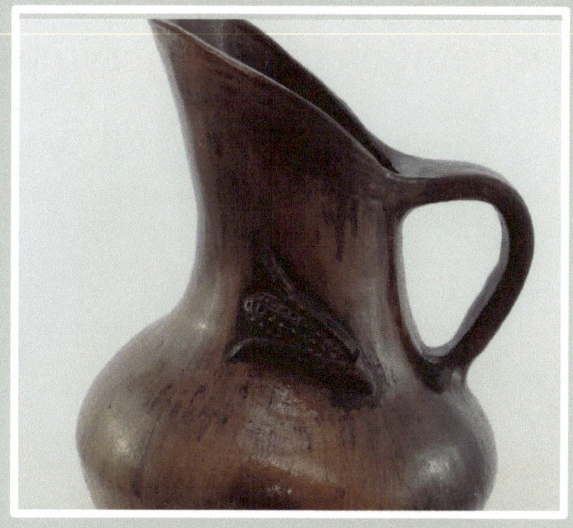

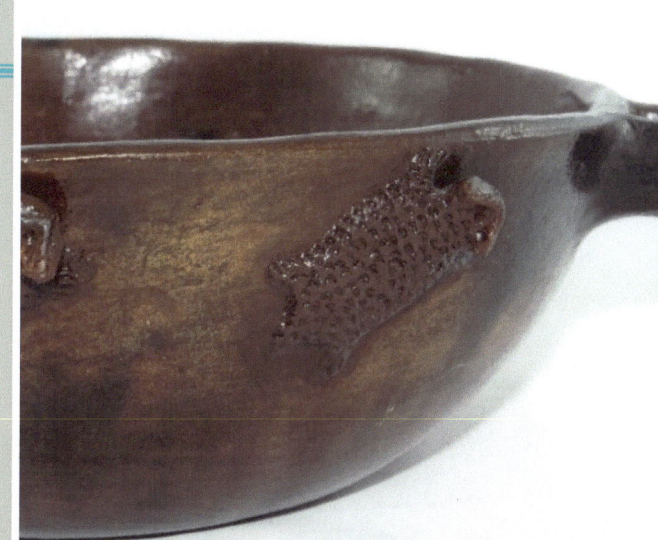

Betty Manygoats   Navajo

Unique Figures – Adding a New Perspective

Instead of just painting visuals on a piece of pottery, the innovators of today are turning the pottery into the figure and adding additional visuals. These are a modern interpretation of ancient symbols.

Although seed jars have been made by pueblo potters for centuries, this one offers a new take on a seed bowl.

This beautiful pot features flowers and delicate hummingbirds.

The sgraffito flowers are inset with turquoise stones in the center of each flower rosette.

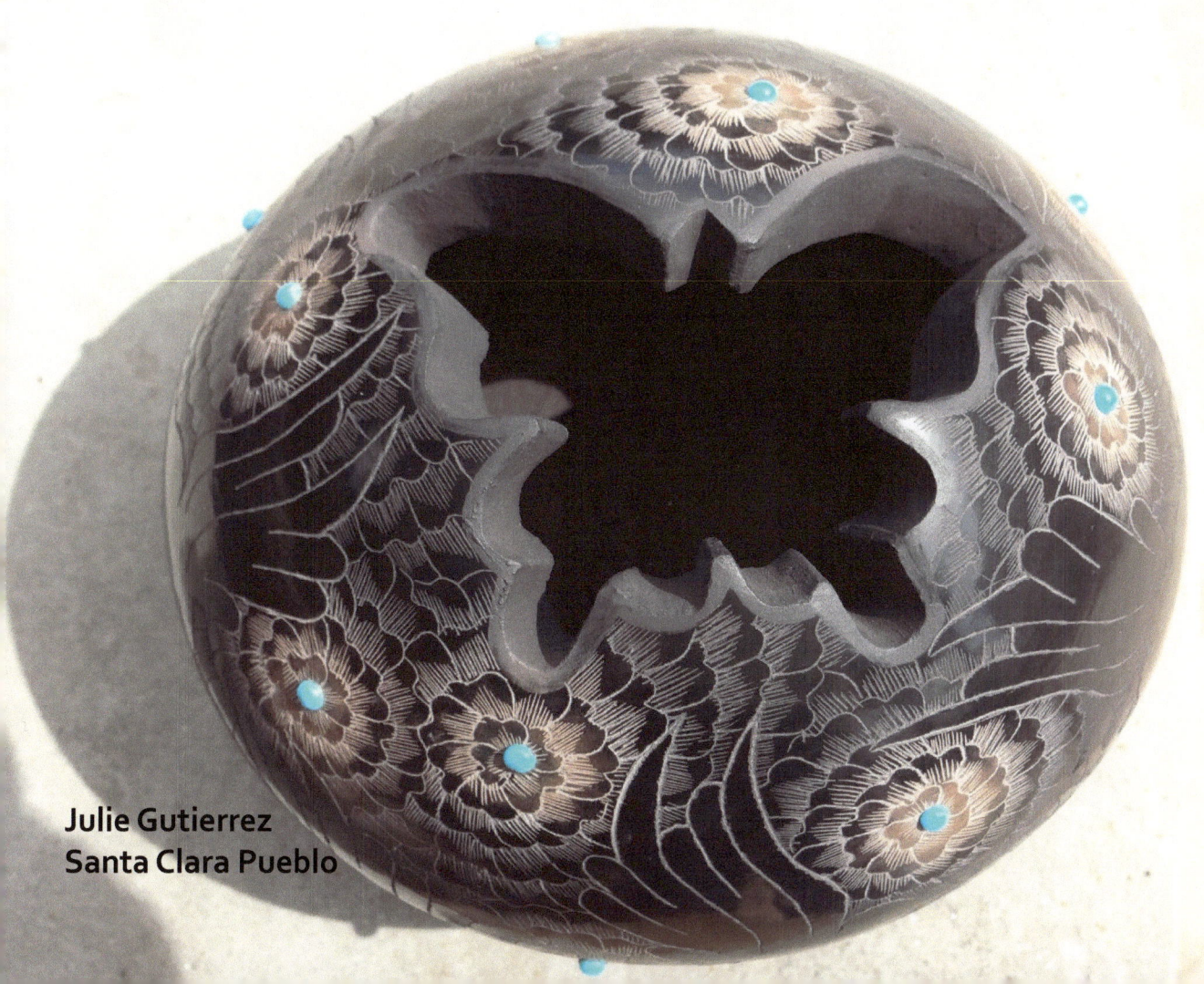

Julie Gutierrez
Santa Clara Pueblo

Traditional and contemporary Zuni designs of rain and lightning, along with the walking deer with the heartline symbol, take on an entirely new aspect when placed on the figure of a duck.

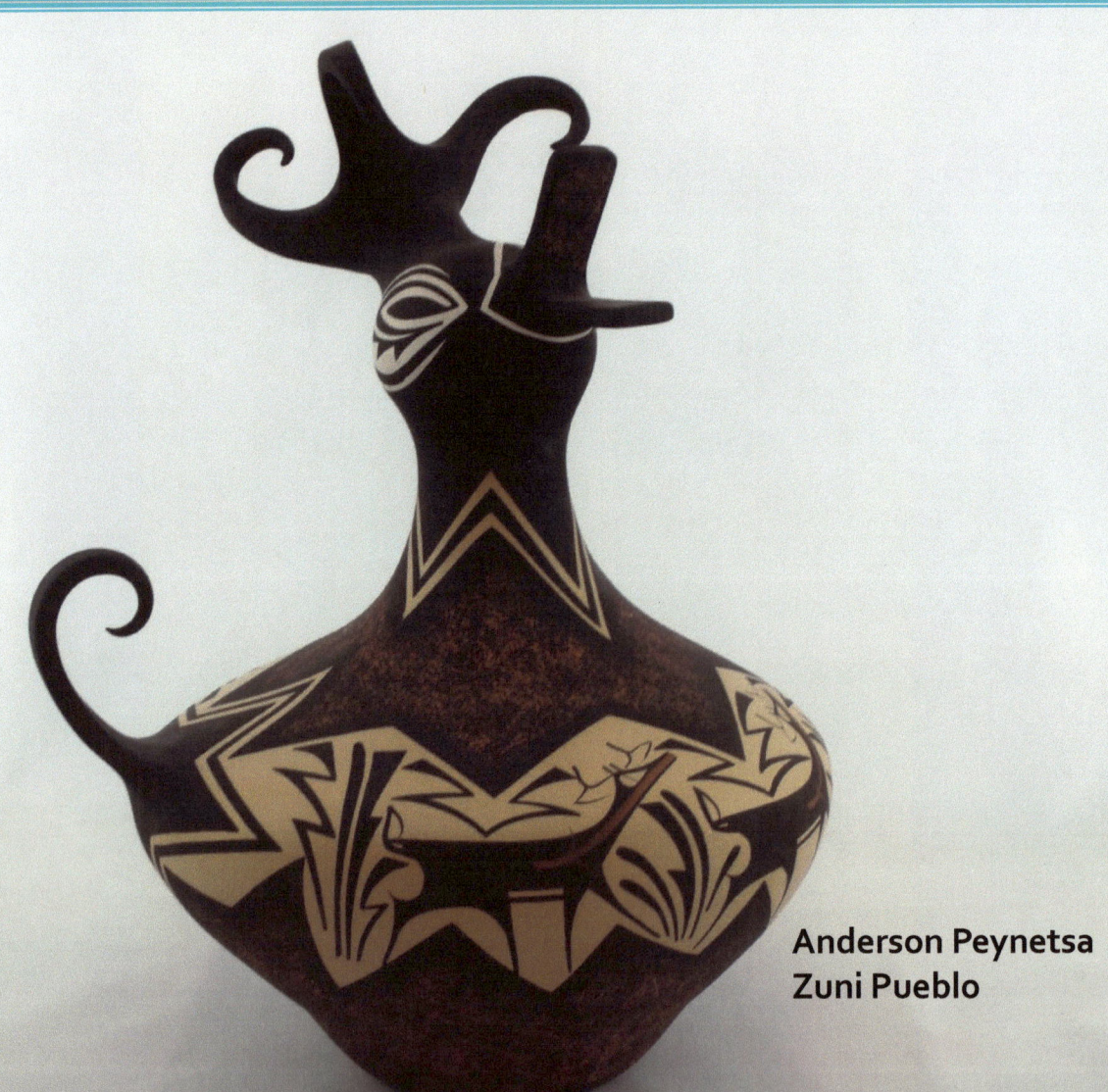

Anderson Peynetsa
Zuni Pueblo

The Zuni owl also takes on an entirely new perspective with the round body and open mouth.

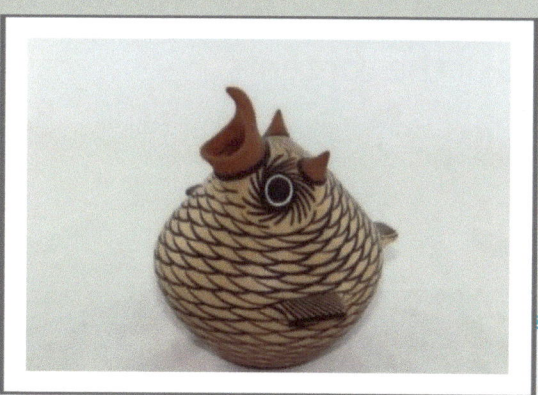

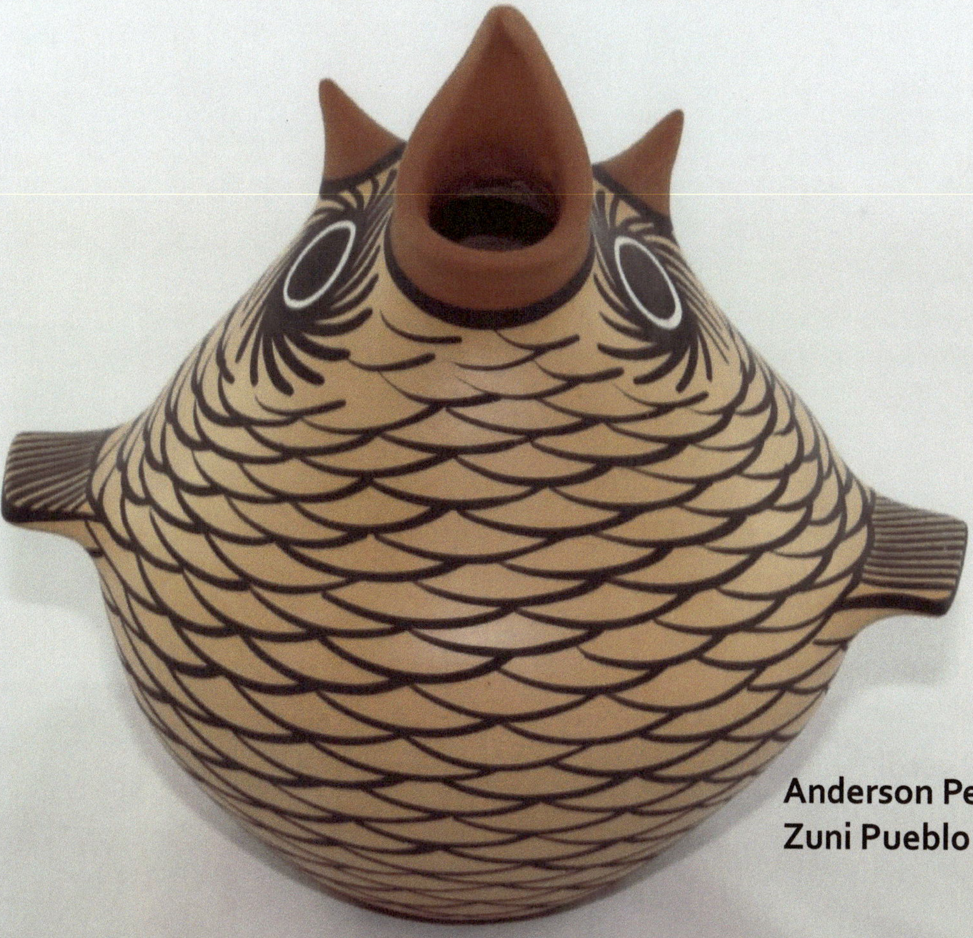

Anderson Peynetsa
Zuni Pueblo

Peering-lizard pots in which the head of a gecko extends over the rim of the pot offer unique guardians of the contents.

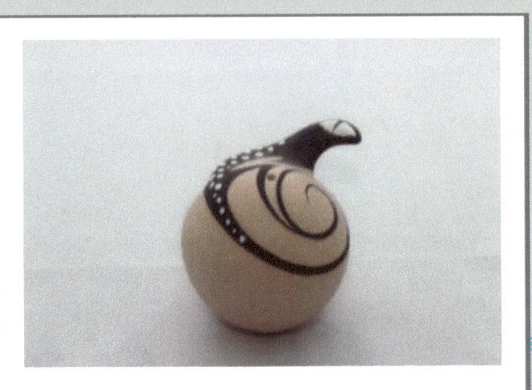

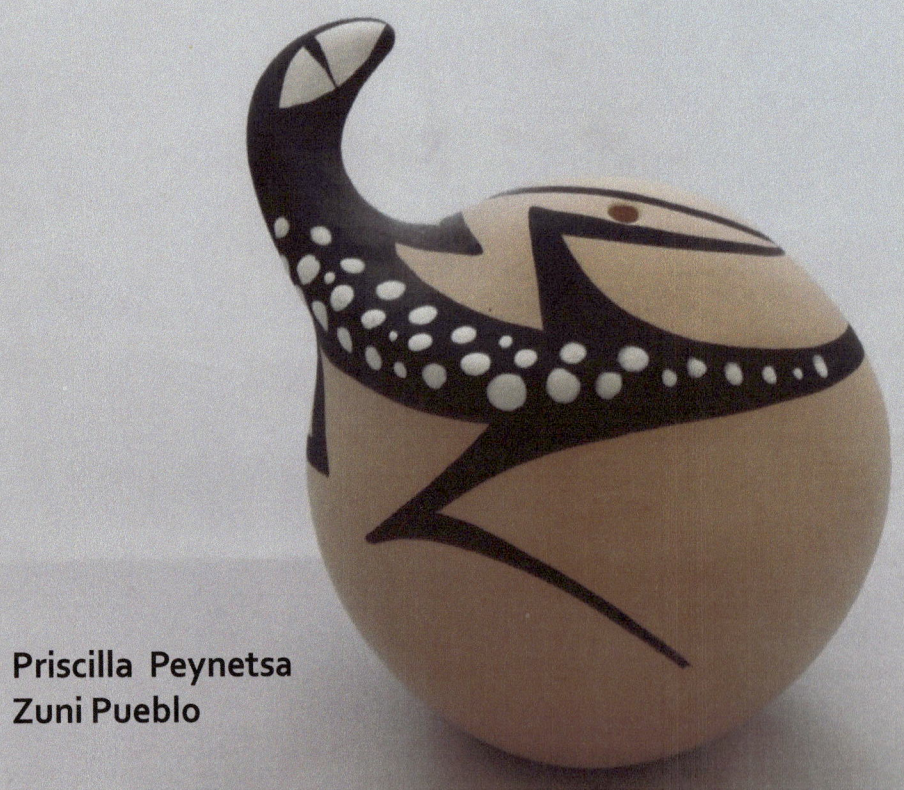

Priscilla Peynetsa
Zuni Pueblo

Intricately detailed 3D lizards elevate this masterpiece with movement.

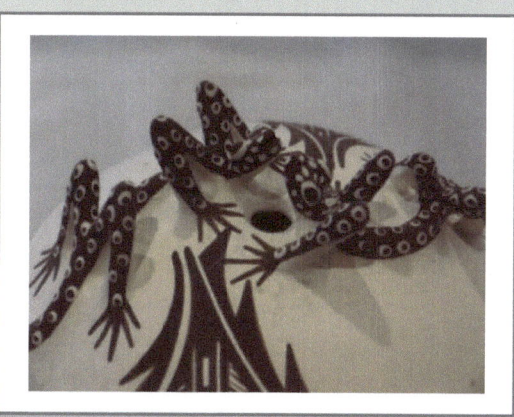

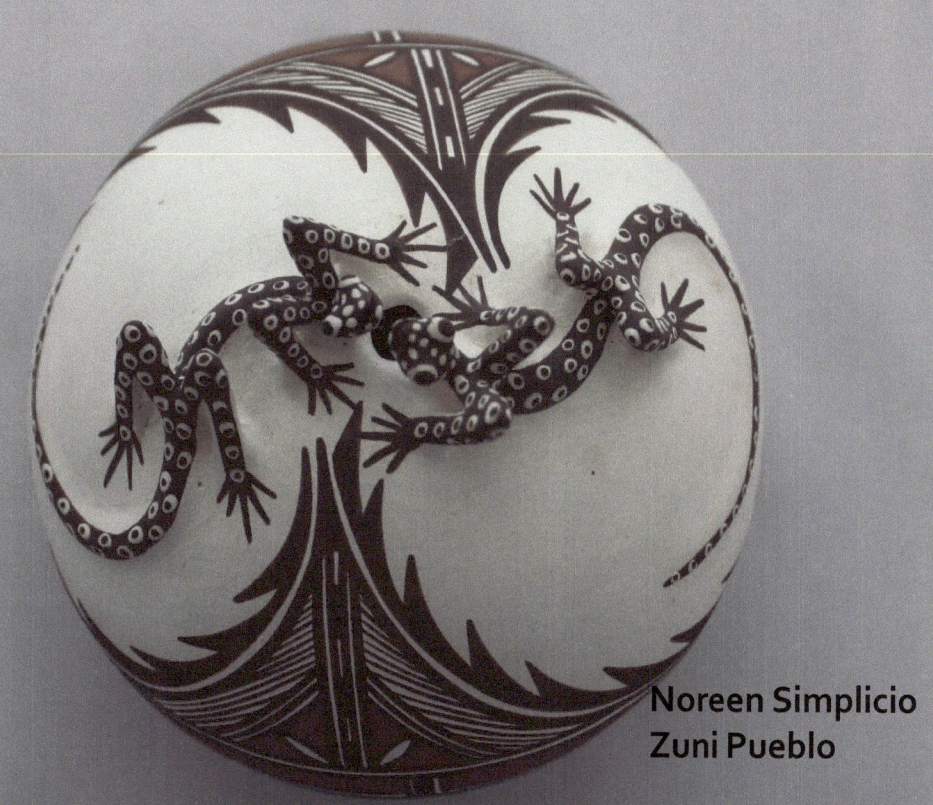

Noreen Simplicio
Zuni Pueblo

The Dancing Rabbit Gallery

AUTHENTIC NATIVE AMERICAN ART

Come Explore
  Online...

thedancingrabbitgallery.com

817-337-8576

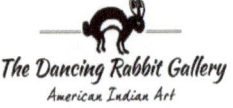

The Dancing Rabbit Gallery
American Indian Art

Founded in 1980   Online since 2012

www.ingramcontent.com/pod-product-compliance
Lightning Source LLC
Chambersburg PA
CBHW042322250526
R18347300001B/R183473PG45473CBX00015B/5